Author:
David Stewart has written many nonfiction
books for children. He lives in Brighton, England,
with his family.

Artist:
David Antram was born in Brighton, England,
in 1958. He studied at Eastbourne College of Art
and then worked in advertising for 15 years before
becoming a full-time artist. He has illustrated many
children's nonfiction books.

Series creator:
David Salariya was born in Dundee,
Scotland. He has illustrated a wide range of books
and has created and designed many new series
for publishers in the UK and overseas. David
established The Salariya Book Company in 1989.
He lives in Brighton with his wife, illustrator
Shirley Willis, and their son, Jonathan.

Editor: **Nick Pierce**

Photo credits:
p.22–23 Sheila Hammer/Shutterstock, Paula
French/Shutterstock, Sam DCruz/Shutterstock,
Sergey Novikov/Shutterstock
p.24–25 Baranov E/Shutterstock, Stu Porter/
Shutterstock, Ondrej Chvatal/Shutterstock, 2020
Photography/Shutterstock, Thoersten Spoerlein/
Shutterstock, Mikadun/Shutterstock, Stefan
Simmerl/Shutterstock

© The Salariya Book Company Ltd MMXXI
No part of this publication may be reproduced, stored in
a retrieval system, or transmitted in any form or by any
means, electronic, mechanical, photocopying, recording,
or otherwise, without written permission of the publisher.
For information regarding permission, write to the
copyright holder.

Published in Great Britain in 2021 by
The Salariya Book Company Ltd
25 Marlborough Place, Brighton BN1 1UB

ISBN 978-0-531-13179-4 (lib. bdg.) 978-0-531-13192-3 (pbk.)

A CIP catalog record for this book is available
from the Library of Congress.

Printed and bound in China.
Printed on paper from sustainable sources.
1 2 3 4 5 6 7 8 9 10 R 28 27 26 25 24 23 22 21

SCHOLASTIC, FRANKLIN WATTS, and associated logos
are trademarks and/or registered trademarks of Scholastic Inc.

Scholastic Inc., 557 Broadway, New York, NY 10012

PAPER FROM
SUSTAINABLE
FORESTS

How Would You Survive as a Lion?

Written by
David Stewart

Illustrated by
David Antram

Series created by
David Salariya

Franklin Watts®
An Imprint of Scholastic Inc.

Contents

You Are a Lion

"King of the beasts" is a great nickname, isn't it? But as a lion, you definitely earn it. You're magnificent: strong, brave, powerful, resourceful, and also wonderful to look at. Your ancestors have inspired writers and artists for thousands of years. All have admired your courage, your skill, and your beauty. In nature, you have few rivals. Other creatures fear you. Over the centuries, your ancestors developed a way of living that has let your species thrive and multiply.

But a lion's life isn't as easy as it seems. You have to survive in a tough climate, compete with other predators for food, and protect your cubs. It's time to answer the big question: How would you survive as a lion?

A Lion's Body

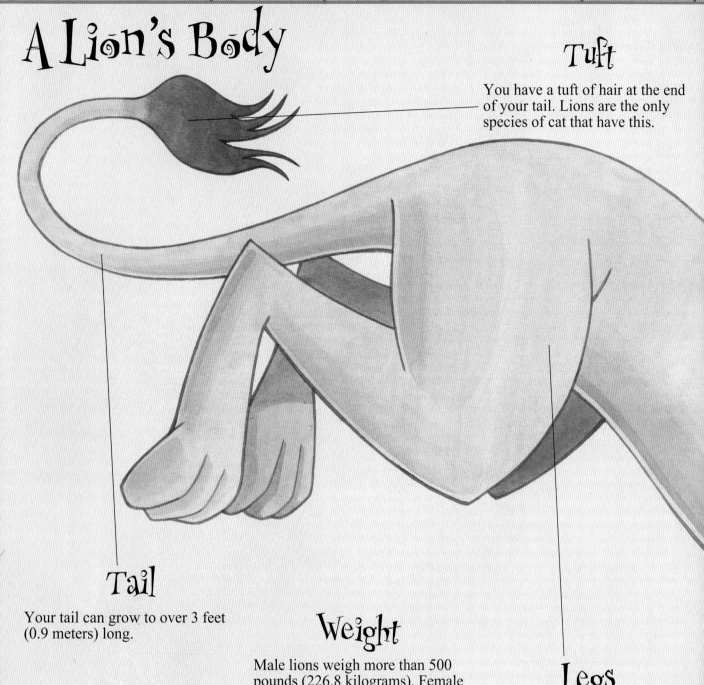

Tuft

You have a tuft of hair at the end of your tail. Lions are the only species of cat that have this.

Tail

Your tail can grow to over 3 feet (0.9 meters) long.

If you are an adult male lion, you would have a mane: thick fur around the neck.

Weight

Male lions weigh more than 500 pounds (226.8 kilograms). Female lions, like you, weigh up to 400 pounds (181.4 kilograms).

Legs

You have very powerful legs. You can reach a top speed of 35 miles per hour (56.3 kilometers per hour), but you cannot maintain this speed for very long periods of time.

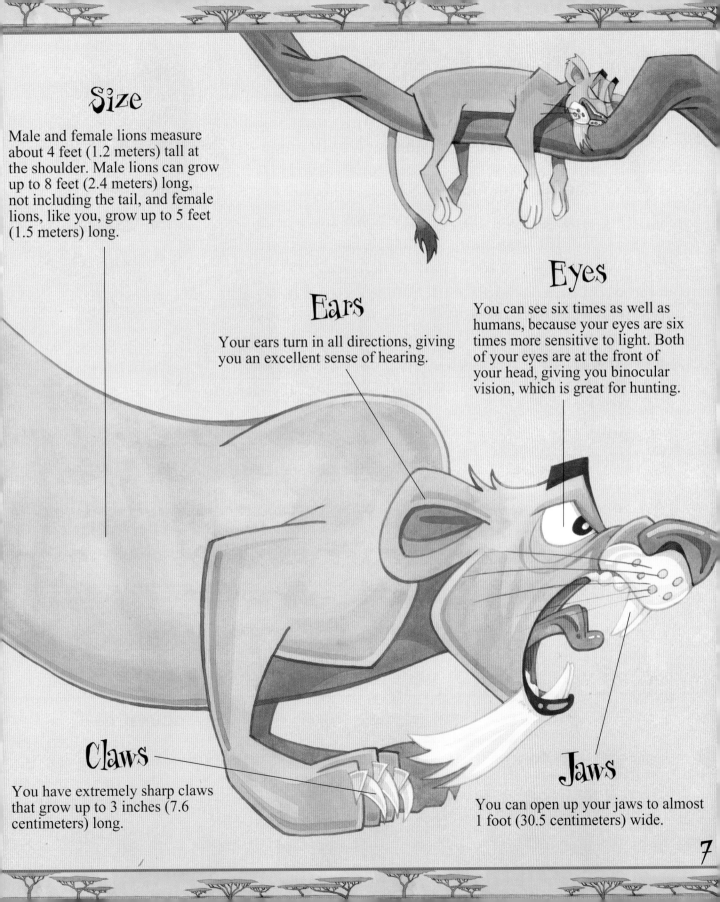

Size

Male and female lions measure about 4 feet (1.2 meters) tall at the shoulder. Male lions can grow up to 8 feet (2.4 meters) long, not including the tail, and female lions, like you, grow up to 5 feet (1.5 meters) long.

Ears

Your ears turn in all directions, giving you an excellent sense of hearing.

Eyes

You can see six times as well as humans, because your eyes are six times more sensitive to light. Both of your eyes are at the front of your head, giving you binocular vision, which is great for hunting.

Claws

You have extremely sharp claws that grow up to 3 inches (7.6 centimeters) long.

Jaws

You can open up your jaws to almost 1 foot (30.5 centimeters) wide.

The African Savanna

Your home, and the home of most lions, is the hot and dry savannas of southern and eastern Africa. There isn't very much vegetation in this habitat—just some shrubs, trees, and tall grasses, which provide good hiding places! There are only two seasons: the dry season and the wet season. In the dry season, water is in short supply. To survive and avoid becoming too dehydrated, you spend most of the day resting and only hunt in the early morning and at dusk when it is cooler. In the wet season, when the rains come, life is a bit easier, and you can fill your belly with water!

If You...

are in an arid area of the savanna with no water, you can get moisture from the stomachs of your prey. Mmm!

▸ In the African savannas, the wet season is hotter and the dry season is cooler.

Ostrich

African spurred tortoise

▾ One tree that thrives in the African savanna is the baobab. This tree can grow up to 164 feet (50 meters) in circumference and live up to 5,000 years!

Dung beetle

▴ The savanna is also home to species of birds, reptiles, and insects like the giant ostrich, the African spurred tortoise, and the poop-loving dung beetle.

Dry season in the savanna

Wet season in the savanna

9

The Pride

Lions are the only big cats to live in groups, called prides. You live in a typical pride made up of three adult males, 15 females, and their cubs. The female lions in a pride are almost always related, usually either sisters or cousins. Your pride splits up into smaller groups during the day to rest, then gathers together again at night to hunt and eat. Sometimes, individual lions can spend many days away from the pride, hunting for food or water. Why do you live in a group? It's less exhausting and there's less chance of injury if you hunt together with others. In short, it's a very good way to survive!

If You...

are a pride male and want to show a member of your pride that you're not happy with them, give them a quick swat with your paw or a gentle bite to the neck.

▶ Lions are pestered by swarms of flies, including the bloodsucking stomoxys. You flick your tail and shake your mane to try to shoo away these pesky insects.

Pride members say hello by rubbing heads and licking. Male lions rub so hard that they can knock each other over!

Your tongue is covered in tiny spines. You use your rough tongue for grooming, to help clean your fur.

The lions in your pride mainly rest during the day, when the heat is most intense. You can all sleep or rest for up to 20 hours of the day!

Home Ground

Another reason why lions live in prides is to defend their home ground. These are areas that lion experts call "hotspots"—territories with the resources that are necessary for survival. Lions often choose to live near rivers, streams, and water holes. This is partly so that they always have access to drinking water, but more importantly, water sources attract prey. When an unsuspecting animal comes to drink, you can pounce. Dinner is served! But if other lions try to muscle in on your turf, you will all have to help fight them off.

If You...

are a male in a lion pride, then look out—you will probably have to defend it against male rivals from other prides, which can end in death or serious injury.

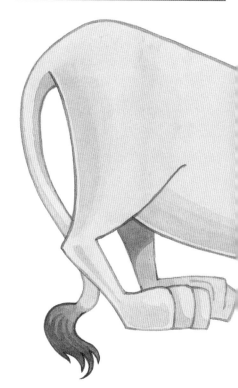

▸ You try to scare off other lions by baring your teeth, showing your claws, standing on your tiptoes, and hunching your back to make yourself look bigger.

▲ You can also let out a loud and terrifying roar to warn other lions to stay out of your territory.

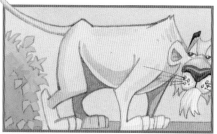

▲ You urinate on the ground and bushes, leaving your scent. This is called territorial marking.

Looks like a lion from another pride is checking out your water hole. You'll have to work together with other members of your pride to scare him off, or there might be trouble!

13

Survival of the Fittest

It is your job, as a female lion, to give birth to and care for new lion cubs. The lionesses in a pride generally give birth at about the same time, and the litter size is usually two to four. When newborn, cubs have a slightly spotted coat, which becomes the same color as their parents' coat after three months. It takes two years to raise a cub to full adulthood. During that time, it is vulnerable, but female lions suckle and care for each other's cubs as well as their own. This communal cub rearing ensures that more cubs will survive to adulthood. But there are many dangers...

If You...

are a male cub, you'll be forced to leave the pride at around the age of three, when the other family members chase you away. You might end up living alone for the rest of your life, or you might join with other males to form a bachelor pride.

Cubs are vulnerable to being eaten by hyenas and leopards, or they can be trampled to death by large animals, like elephants.

If a lioness is worried about the safety of her cubs, she can gently pick them up in her mouth and transport them to a safer place.

If another group of male lions take over a pride, they may kill all of the cubs so that the lionesses can have their cubs instead.

Hunting

Y ou hunt and eat other living creatures to survive. Lionesses are better hunters than male lions because they are faster and more agile. You use teamwork to catch your prey. First, you sneak up on your prey as a group. You look for weak, sick, or young animals that are easier to bring down. Once you've chosen, one lioness chases the poor animal toward the other lionesses. They all jump on it, biting and slashing with their claws. Finally, one lioness kills it with a bite to the neck or snout.

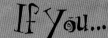

If You...

are wondering what humans think about lions, you should know that lions are very common in heraldry, where they often symbolize courage, strength, and royalty.

◀ You will get as close as possible to your prey by hiding in the grass and slowly creeping up, before suddenly charging.

▼ You hunt wildebeests, zebras, waterbucks, kudu, antelope, and also animals that are bigger than them, like buffalo and giraffes.

Wildebeest *Zebra* *Waterbuck* *Kudu* *Buffalo*

18

Natural Hazards

Although you're a big and fearsome predator, you're not immortal. Lions frequently face death or serious injury from other animals and the invisible threat of disease. Some of the most formidable competitors for a lion are packs of hyenas. These dangerous predators can use teamwork to intimidate a lion away from its fresh kill. You're no innocent victim, though—lions are equally given to stealing hyenas' freshly caught prey. It's safe to say that there is no love lost between these two deadly species of African predators! You'll need to learn to respect the hazard posed by the other predators in the savanna if you're going to survive!

If You...

are drinking at the edge of a lake or water hole, be careful you don't become the prey of another big predator: a crocodile! It could grab you in its jaws and drag you under!

▼ Getting injured during a hunt can be a serious problem. If the wound stops you from hunting, you may starve to death. If it gets infected, you might die.

▼ You are vulnerable to illnesses like canine distemper, which causes flu-like symptoms, and feline immunodeficiency virus, which can cause your muscles to waste away.

Threats From Humans

I t's not just the natural world that has its dangers. You're also at risk from human activity. Lions have been hunted and killed for trophies or as symbols of bravery for hundreds of years, and caught to be sold into captivity. Poachers kill lions illegally in order to sell their fur and other body parts for use as decorations or ingredients in traditional forms of medicine. Farmers in parts of Africa also sometimes kill lions in order to protect their livestock from being eaten. Lions are now a protected species, but many are still killed every year.

If You...

were a lion in a zoo in the past, you probably would've had a miserable time. Although zoos now prioritize conservation, in the early 20th century, animals like lions were kept in tiny cages and treated as curiosities.

Some of the Dangers:

Traditional healers in African and Chinese medicine use parts of lions to treat their customers.

Many lions have been killed, both in the past and in the present day, to keep up with the demand for trophy hunting.

Some lions have been made to perform tricks in circus acts for paying audiences, which many now see as cruel.

Lions have been captured in the wild with nets and sold to private collectors.

Poachers will often pose for photographs with the lions and other animals that they have killed.

The Story of Cecil the Lion

You might be at the top of the food chain, but as we've seen, surviving as a lion is still full of dangers. There are many stories of lions that highlight some of the conservation issues they face, and one is the happy life and the sad death of Cecil the lion, who made news headlines around the world in 2015.

1. Cecil the lion lived in Zimbabwe's Hwange National Park and was popular with tourists.

2. Cecil was the leader of two prides, along with another lion named Jericho. The prides contained six lionesses and 12 cubs.

3. He was recognizable because of his large size and shaggy black mane.

GPS collar

4. Cecil was being studied by lion conservation researchers. They place GPS collars on lions so that they can track their movements.

5. When he was 13 years old, Cecil was killed by a trophy hunter. It is believed he was lured out of Hwange National Park at night and killed. His death highlights the problem of lion trophy hunting, which results in the deaths of many lions every year. Governments and international organizations are working to combat poaching and wildlife smuggling.

Lion Family Tree

Lions are part of the Felidae family of animals, also called cats. All of these species have a common ancestor that lived around 14 million years ago. All of these different species are carnivores, meaning that they eat other animals in order to survive. If you were a lion, these would be some of your closest cousins...

Lynx

These cats have big, furry paws that allow them to walk in the snow, since they live in cold climates.

Mountain Lion

A type of lion found in America. They are usually solitary hunters.

Cheetah

This type of cat can run faster than any other animal that lives on the land.

Leopard

This species is known for the distinctive markings on its body.

Lion (You)

Lions are recognizable by the manes that the males of the species have around their heads. They usually live together in family groups called prides.

Tiger

These are the largest species of cat. They have dark stripes across their fur coats.

Jaguar

This is the largest species of big cat to live in South America.

Lion Quiz

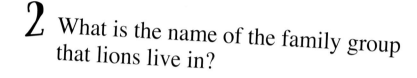

1 What is it called when lions use their rough tongues to help clean each other's fur?

2 What is the name of the family group that lions live in?

3 What is it called when lions urinate on the ground and bushes to warn other lions to stay away from their home?

4 How long does it take to raise a lion cub to full adulthood?

5 What is the name for a pride made up only of male lions?

6 What predator can sometimes attack lions drinking at a water hole?

7 From what can lions obtain moisture in an arid area of the savanna?

8 If another group of male lions take over a pride, what might they do?

9 What is the name of the disease that causes muscles to waste away in lions?

10 What do lions show off when they feel threatened?

Lion Quiz Answers

1 Grooming
(page 10)

2 A pride
(page 10)

3 Territorial marking
(page 12)

4 Two years
(page 15)

5 Bachelor pride
(page 15)

6 Crocodile
(page 19)

7 Stomachs of their prey
(page 8)

8 Kill all of the cubs
(page 15)

9 Feline immunodeficiency virus
(page 19)

10 Their teeth and claws
(page 12)

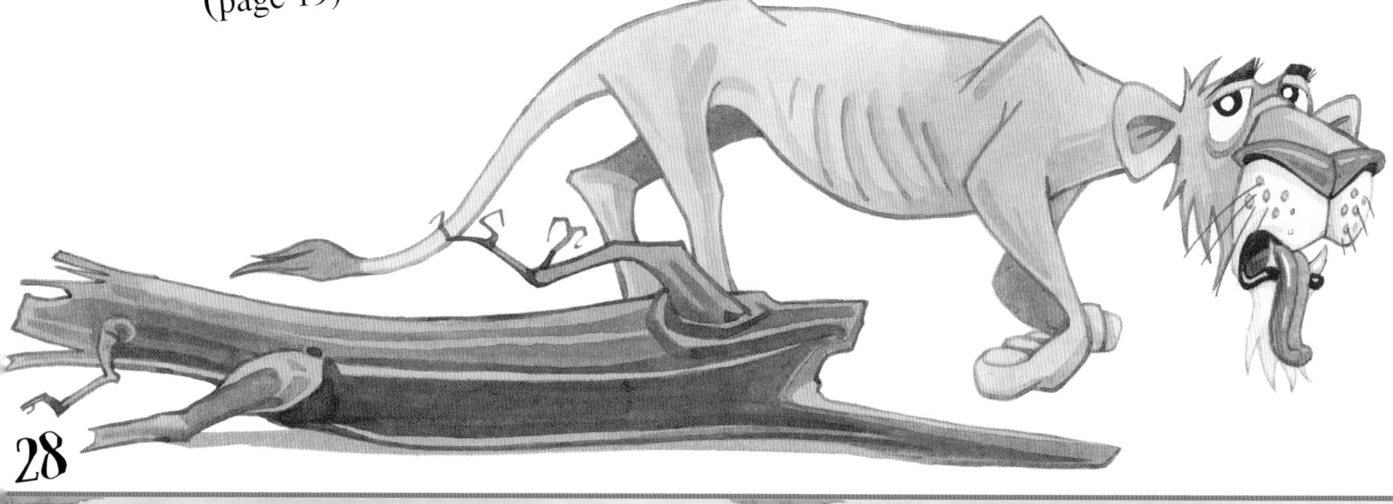

Lion Facts

There are only 20,000 African lions left in the wild. The species was classified as "vulnerable" in 1996 by the IUCN (International Union for Conservation of Nature).

Only a single lioness and her cub lived in Botswana's Selinda area before it was turned into a protected reserve for the animals. Now there are 100 lions living in the reserve.

Occasionally, a female lion will grow a mane. No one knows the reason for this!

Due to reduced living space and conflict with people, lion numbers have dropped by 43% in two decades.

Lions have a less than 30% success rate at hunting.

10% of the world's remaining lion population live in Ruaha National Park in Tanzania.

Lions live for 10 to 18 years in the wild, and up to 30 years in captivity.

The largest ever relocation of lions saw 24 lions moved from South Africa to Mozambique's Zambezi Delta, where lion numbers had dropped dramatically as a result of a civil war in the area.

Where Do Big Cats Live?

There are cat species living on every continent on the planet, except for Antarctica. The map below describes where lions and other species of big cats live in the wild.

Mountain lions are native to the Americas. There are still several thousand in the wild, mainly located in the western United States.

Lions live in the grasslands and forests of India and sub-Saharan Africa.

Leopards are found across Africa and Asia, including in Kenya, Zimbabwe, India, Afghanistan, and China.

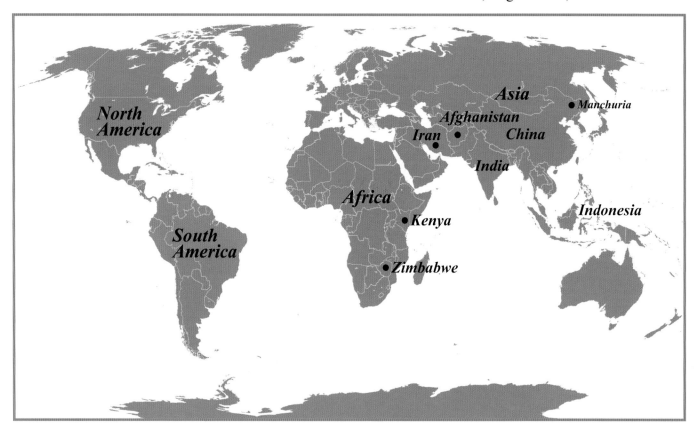

Tigers live across a wide variety of habitats. The Bengal tiger is found in India, the Amur tiger in Manchuria, and the South China and Indochinese tigers in China. The Sumatran tiger can be seen in Indonesia.

Cheetahs live in eastern and southern Africa. There is also a small population in Iran.

Glossary

Agile The ability to move quickly and with great physical ease.

Ancestors The animals that lived in the past from which a modern species of animal is descended.

Binocular vision The capacity to focus on a single object with both eyes and see a single visual image.

Captivity When an animal is confined to a small space by humans rather than being allowed to roam freely.

Communal When something, such as a job, is shared by all of the members of a particular community.

Conservation Protecting animal and plant species from extinction.

Dehydrated When you do not have enough water in your body for it to carry out its normal functions.

Heraldry The system of designing coats of arms used by individuals, families, countries, or companies.

Immortal Something or someone that can live forever.

Litter A group of several young animals born to a mother at one time.

Livestock Species of animals such as cows or sheep that are raised by farmers to provide goods such as meat, milk, or wool.

Poaching Hunting and killing animals illegally, usually to sell their body or skin for profit.

Savanna An ecosystem of mixed woodland and grassland. In a savanna, the trees are spaced wide enough apart so that light reaches the ground everywhere.

Solitary A human or animal that lives on its own.

Index